PAINFUL PARASITES

by
Charis Mather

Minneapolis, Minnesota

Credits

Images are courtesy of Shutterstock.com. With thanks to GettyImages, ThinkstockPhoto, and iStockphoto.

Cover – GoodFocused, nechaevkon, Vector_Up. Recurring images – gravity_point, yugoro, The_Pixel, Iyeyee, Voin_Sveta, nataliiudina, ozzichka, MarShot. 2–3 – Francesco_Ricciardi. 4–5 – Bilanol, kosmos111. 6–7 – KanphotoSS, Mi St, Silarock. 8–9 – Kateryna Kon, Todorean-Gabriel. 10–11 – khunkornStudio, kwanchai.c, SciePro. 12–13 – Diaz Aragon, Scott Bauer (Wikimedia Commons), Keegan Morrison (Wikimedia Commons). 14–15 – Ayah Raushan, ijimino. 16–17 – Amelia Tauber (Wikimedia Commons), Peddalanka Ramesh Babu, Tacio Philip Sansonovski. 18–19 – EVGEIIA, Quang nguyen vinh, suprabhat. 20–21 – Denis Vesely, Kevin Wells Photography, sergio34. 22–23 – devil79sd, JPC-PROD, SB Arts Media.

Library of Congress Cataloging-in-Publication Data

Names: Mather, Charis, 1999- author.
Title: Painful parasites / by Charis Mather.
Description: Minneapolis, Minnesota : Bearport Publishing Company, [2024] | Series: Beastly wildlife | Includes index.
Identifiers: LCCN 2023031021 (print) | LCCN 2023031022 (ebook) | ISBN 9798889163411 (hardcover) | ISBN 9798889163466 (paperback) | ISBN 9798889163503 (ebook)
Subjects: LCSH: Parasites--Juvenile literature.
Classification: LCC QL757 .M338 2024 (print) | LCC QL757 (ebook) | DDC 591.7/857--dc23/eng/20230714
LC record available at https://lccn.loc.gov/2023031021
LC ebook record available at https://lccn.loc.gov/2023031022

© 2024 BookLife Publishing
This edition is published by arrangement with BookLife Publishing.

North American adaptations © 2024 Bearport Publishing Company. All rights reserved. No part of this publication may be reproduced in whole or in part, stored in any retrieval system, or transmitted in any form or by any means, electronic, mechanical, photocopying, recording, or otherwise, without written permission from the publisher.

For more information, write to Bearport Publishing, 5357 Penn Avenue South, Minneapolis, MN 55419.

CONTENTS

Beastly!	4
Frightful Fleas	6
Unwelcome Worms	8
Lousy Lice	10
Worrisome Wasps	12
Tasteless Tongue-Eaters	14
Beastly Botfly Larvae	16
Plant Parasites	18
Not-So-Fun Fungi	20
Painfully Parasitic Pests	22
Glossary	24
Index	24

Parasites are creatures that need to live off **hosts** to survive. These awful critters use their hosts as homes and for food, and they give nothing in return. Parasites are pretty beastly, but you can't really blame them for wanting somewhere to live.

FRIGHTFUL FLEAS

Fleas are small **insects** that live on the skin and fur of other animals. They bite their hosts to drink blood for a tasty meal. *Slurp!* Flea bites can be very itchy.

These tiny parasites are excellent jumpers. Fleas use their strong back legs to jump many times their own height. This makes it easy for them to hop aboard a host.

UNWELCOME WORMS

Some parasites are great at worming their way into new homes... literally! There are many types of parasitic worms that live inside the guts of other animals. But how do they get there?

Threadworms, hookworms, and tapeworms are sometimes found inside humans.

A tapeworm

A threadworm

A hookworm

The worms are eaten! Some food, such as uncooked meat, can be **infested** with tiny worm eggs. After animals eat the food, the parasite eggs **hatch** inside them and grow into long worms. The wiggly beasts can go unnoticed for years!

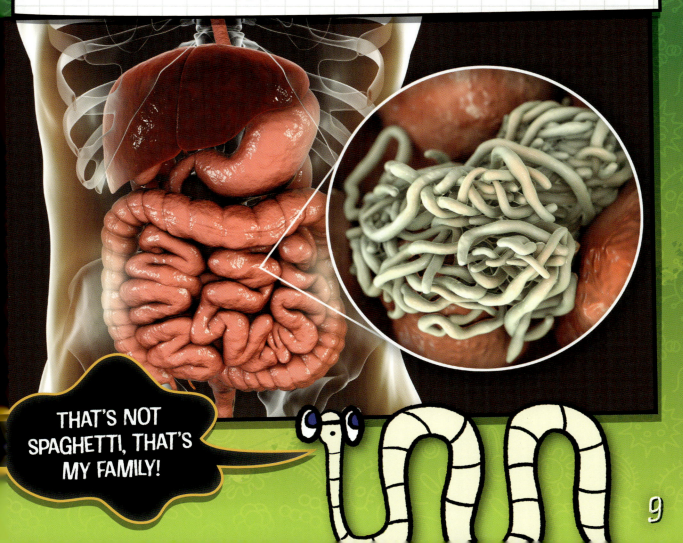

THAT'S NOT SPAGHETTI, THAT'S MY FAMILY!

LOUSY LICE

If you are scratching your head more than usual, it might be because of lice. These little critters live on human hair. They drink blood from a host's scalp, and their bites can be very itchy. *Scratch, scratch!*

LICE TO MEET YOU!

Adult lice can live for about 30 days on your hair, eyebrows, and even on your eyelashes.

These small parasites are often hard to spot. The adults are about the size of a sesame seed and move quickly. They spend their lives feeding and laying tiny eggs that look like flakes of dry skin.

WORRISOME WASPS

EGG DELIVERY!

Some wasps are parasites that are both painful and deadly for their hosts. These buzzing creatures lay their eggs on or in caterpillars, spiders, and other critters. Once the eggs hatch, wasp **larvae** eat their hosts alive. *Yum!*

Some of these larvae turn their hosts into **zombies** to control their bodies before killing them. One type even forces host spiders to spin cocoons. There, the larvae can safely grow into adult wasps.

SHARING IS CARING!

TASTELESS TONGUE-EATERS

The tongue-eating louse works hard to earn its name. But you don't need to worry about this weird parasite eating you. It feeds on fish tongues!

I'M AN EXCELLENT TASTE BUDDY!

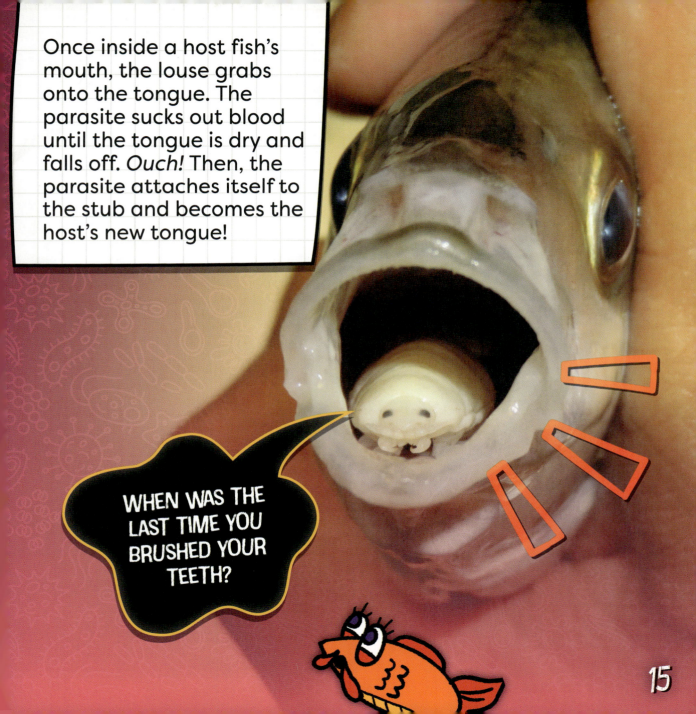

Once inside a host fish's mouth, the louse grabs onto the tongue. The parasite sucks out blood until the tongue is dry and falls off. *Ouch!* Then, the parasite attaches itself to the stub and becomes the host's new tongue!

WHEN WAS THE LAST TIME YOU BRUSHED YOUR TEETH?

BEASTLY BOTFLY LARVAE

Botflies might look harmless, but these insects have a truly beastly start to life. Botfly larvae grow under the skin of other animals . . . including humans!

An adult botfly

A botfly larva

Watch out! Botfly larvae dig into their living homes with hook-shaped mouthparts. They spend up to three months buried under a creature's skin. The parasites feed on their host's flesh until they are ready to pop out.

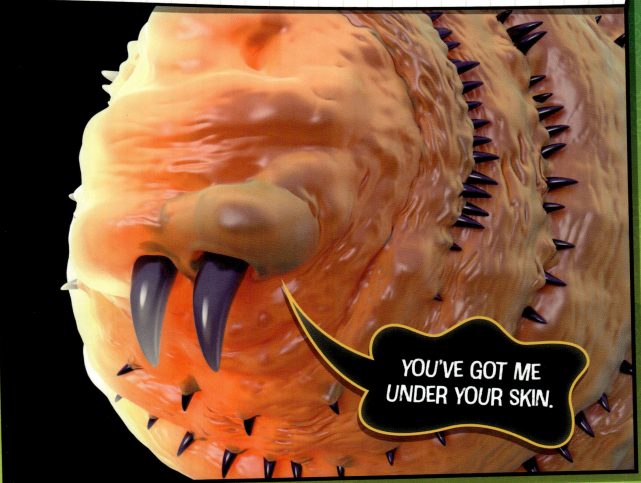

PLANT PARASITES

Host

Dodder looks like a big pile of spaghetti.

Plants can be parasites, too! Unlike most plants, the dodder does not get food from the sun. Instead, it sucks food from a host plant.

This parasitic **vine** curls tightly around a plant. Then, parts of the vine poke into the host to steal food. *Yikes!* This makes the host plant weaker and less healthy.

NOBODY WORRY, EVERYTHING IS VINE.... I MEAN FINE!

NOT-SO-FUN FUNGI

The cordyceps **fungus** can grow only when it's about 10 inches (25 cm) off the ground. How does it get there without legs? This parasite turns host ants into zombies to do the climbing for them.

The cordyceps fungus is also called the zombie-ant fungus.

DO YOU WANT TO BE FRIENDS?

When a fungus **spore** lands on an ant, the parasite spreads inside and takes control of the insect's body. It makes its host climb to a good spot. Then, it bursts out of the host's head, spreading more spores.

A cordyceps fungus

PAINFULLY PARASITIC PESTS

Many parasites seem like something straight out of a scary story. Some are painful, some are gross, and some can even be deadly.

These weird critters are super interesting. Still, that doesn't mean you want to have a parasite yourself. After all, they are pretty beastly!

GLOSSARY

fungus a plantlike thing, such as a mushroom, that can't make its own food

hatch to come out of an egg

hosts animals or plants that parasites live on or feed from

infested filled with harmful creatures

insects small animals that have six legs and three main body parts

larvae the wormlike form of many kinds of young insects

spore a tiny part of fungus that is able to grow into new fungus

vine a plant that grows by climbing up something else

zombies creatures that act or look dead and have no control of their bodies

INDEX

bite 6, 10
blood 6, 10, 15
eggs 9, 11–12
food 4–5, 9, 18–19
guts 8

hair 10–11
larvae 12–13, 16–17
plants 18–19
skin 6, 11, 16–17
tongues 14–15